Fire Eater

Fire Eater

poems by

Kathleen Jesme

UNIVERSITY OF TAMPA PRESS • TAMPA, FLORIDA • 2003

Manufactured in the United States of America
Cover and book design by Richard Mathews
Printed on acid-free paper
First Edition

University of Tampa Press
401 West Kennedy Blvd.
Tampa, FL 33606

ISBN 1-879852-85-3 (pbk)
ISBN 1-879852-88-8 (cloth)

Browse & order online at
http://utpress.ut.edu

Library of Congress Cataloging-in-Publication Data

Jesme, Kathleen.
  Fire eater : poems / by Kathleen Jesme.
    p. cm.
  ISBN 1-879852-85-3 (pbk. : alk. paper)
  1. Minnesota—Poetry. 2. Fires—Poetry. I. Title.
  PS3610.E86 F57 2003
  811'.6—dc21
                                2003001136

For A.H., J.S., and C.L.W.

Contents

1

The Arsonist • 1

Fire Eater • 3

The Trees Turn • 4

Persephone's Sister • 5

1910 • 7

At Eight, When the House Burned • 21

April Day • 22

Red Shift • 23

Depth of Field • 29

2

Let Them • 33

Afraid to Look Afraid to Look Away • 34

Has Been Seen • 36

September Frost Warning • 37

The Bare Minimum • 42

From Home • 43

Source • 44

On Two ▪ 45

Divided ▪ 48

3

Amherst Winter ▪ 51

Conversation with My Father ▪ 56

Novitiate ▪ 58

Landscape: Western Minnesota ▪ 64

Winter Necessities ▪ 65

Ripening ▪ 66

Fireflies ▪ 67

Notes ▪ 69

Acknowledgments ▪ 70

About the Author ▪ 71

About the Book ▪ 73

*Make no mistake: There's fire
back where you came from, too.*

▪ Rita Dove

The Arsonist

The long fall grass bends toward her, yellowed
in the wind, waves her on.
It rises

above her on the hillside, almost to the houses,
and slopes below to the river
where the water's gray fists chop the whirring air.

She rips out handfuls of straw and weeds, piles them up
half her height. The wind wants
to take them

but she holds them down with her lunchbox. What she sees
is not what is here: a small
contained fire over which to toast hot dogs and bread.

What she sees out of the narrow frame of childhood
is a landscape smaller
and safer

than anything she really knows. The eye
of her imagination
diminishes

whatever becomes monstrous,
whatever is dangerous,
so that

she can find its place in herself without terror.
And so she doesn't know
what will happen

when she kneels aside the wind to strike
the match.
How the grass will catch—

how the wind will take the fire
and tangle and toss it
up the hill.

And she will not be able to stop it.
It will never stop
becoming fire.

And try as she might, she will never be able
to remember it
quite right—

the way the fire truck sounds with its Doppler roar
and the soft swish of voices on the streets
as the news passes,

and later, the thought of burning up
with the grass,
how easy it would have been,

and the way the hill
becomes a black patch of shame she can't look at
until snow comes and covers it.

Fire Eater

for C.D.

In first grade he sat in front of me
and I could watch the white, angry ropes
of flesh on his hands, his cheeks,
the back of his neck, examine
the bare places on his head where hair
wouldn't grow. I became used

to the odd way his head tilted and nodded
when he walked, a little sideways,
as if something were always pulling or pushing
him. I wondered if the same fire
had melted the rest of him, the parts
I couldn't see: his skinny arms
and thighs, his back. I wondered
if any of him were smooth.

When Mrs. Smith held him on her lap
though he wanted to get down, he kicked her
because that was all he could do,
and that sweet teacher took him
into the classroom alone and raged
and raged at him—and I walked by
twice because I needed to know what she
could do: Even the boy, that burned,
scarred, trembling boy,
could be burned some more,
and would be.

The Trees Turn

October's fiery sun enters the woods
    falls down among the trees
    spatters the ground.

Looking west I see the heart of the woods:
    a furnace of light.

You tell me to enter this light—or is it this heart,
    this woods, this furnace?

But if I stand here and wait a while
    until it enters me—

No, surely it will pass by
    just as you have
    without igniting

even though the fuel is dry
    and ready for flame.

Persephone's Sister

I was the extra one, not the daughter
my mother moved heaven and earth
to find again. I was the one

who picked the flower inside Aunt Anna's rotten tree stump,
my sister didn't do that, but she was the one
who was lost.

They said my mother turned the earth inside out to find
her: I only know earth
was cold and vacant most of the time.

I remember once, being caught in a thicket of young poplars
so dense I couldn't slip between them
and thought I would die there

in that young woods. She was moving heaven and earth
to find my sister. The bones in my fingers get heavy,
remembering.

We used to play hide and seek, long summer
evenings, until the sky went down at ten o'clock,
and I always hid inside the canoe

tipped up on sawhorses. I would get up in the canoe,
stretch myself across the gunnels,
no one ever found me

because you had to look under
and then up
to see me in the contracting dark.

Summer came and went and my sister
never really returned despite all the deals
my mother made with

the greening of things.
I spent winter afternoons listening
to sea chanties on the record player.

Once, I burned Munson's Hill
trying to roast hot dogs on a fire in long grass,
windy, dry day. And once

He saw me. We looked
at each other. I could have told,
but I had already forgotten.

Time went by and my mother
continued
to be away—

But I, looking in the mirror this morning,
see that I have come up from
the house

of lightlessness, even so.

1910

1. One Year Later

The trees still line the hill, branches mostly gone,
odd angles to the horizon. The sky seems still filled with smoke,
dense and dusty. The flag, at half mast, barely shows
through opaque air. It disappears with the bare treetops.
Hundreds of people circle the mass grave; it is so hard
to remember. They stand in knots and clusters and lines,
disorganized, trickling down the hill toward the trench, its scar
visible, dirt heaped like a giant mole tunnel
along the riverbank. The man in the foreground
isn't much bigger than the others, but he is noticeable
from the back because of how he holds his left arm,
elbow up, as if his fingers were wiping his eyes.
His right hand holds his hat behind his back,
so that it forms a bowl, like a basin, empty, waiting to be filled.

2. All the Trees

became lumber or tinder—
Norway pine, white pine,
   white cedar,
white spruce, black spruce,
   tamarack,
jack pine, popple, Balm of Gilead,
   balsam fir,
bur oak, red oak,
   paper birch, green ash,
American elm,
   box elder—
forests of black poles,
dense carpets of ash.

3. Countless Peat Fires

The bog is burning:
through September's sun it flares

and simmers.
No rain since May:
the peat smolders.

Some say the railroad
started the fires, sparks
flying off the metal wheels
and kindling the dust,
or coal engines without protective screening
spouting cinders over dry grass.

Everywhere the ground is on fire,
condensed in the verge of October wind.
And the earth quickens.

4. The Root Cellar

*Over 50 people are gathered in the shack
of Wm. Monroe, a few miles south of Clementson,
who are living on potatoes baked in the fire.*
–"The Rainy River Region," Oct. 13, 1910

It has been so dry: All summer
    we try to irrigate
the kitchen garden. Mother and I dig shallow ditches
between the rows, haul bucket
    after bucket of water
from the well, but everything
        is small and dusty,

so we leave it all in the ground into October, hoping
for some miracle.
    The rain never comes. Potatoes
like pebbles, marble-sized onions, carrots slim and pale
still slicing down into the hard ground, their tops gray
and weepy: everywhere the smell of dust and dirt.

    When it comes, the fire sparks the red maple trees.
Small fires already burn
    everywhere in the county.
        We are at school—
a boy named Nels looks out the window and says,

    "There's a fire."
        Nobody listens. He says, "This fire is coming fast!"
    Miss Larson goes to the window:
It is bellowing in the trees, leaping across the tracks.

She tells us to grab our coats and books and run.
                        We look back
and see the schoolhouse burning along with the treetops.
We run as fast as we can.
                At home,
Father is fighting cinders on the house roof
    with wet blankets, but soon
                    the wave of fire
spills over the house from the southwest:

                We retreat
to the empty root cellar with wet blankets and faces
muffled by cloth, tears
and the weight of hot air.

The root cellar is musty and empty, end of season.
Nothing much left but a few old potatoes, black
and wrinkled, fingers poking out
                every which way.
At first, it smells of dry dirt
    and potatoes right at the edge of spoiling.
Then it smells oppressive, like singed hair—

The cellar is ringed with glowing light
    that catches the translucent potato fingers
and turns them rose-colored.

When we come up
earth's oven
has sealed the dark air.

5. The Church Bells

Red hot in the fire's forge, all the bells
have fallen now,
clappers melted to their sides.

They came down pealing
as if to announce
the end of war. The whole town rang.

Morning comes with a sugary dust
of snow. There is nothing
for the wind

to speak to—no trees, no corners,
nothing but the chimneys
standing row by row.

6. David Coutts

6 Thursday.
Wind freshning. Smoke
has me nearly blind. Fire raging, early night
I went to Maggie's house and took out
what things I was able to carry
to clearing. At dark
I made two trips. Trees falling
and fire.

7 Friday.
Had to cut our way in.
Fire still growing. Someone died,
could not get out no way.
Fire balls lighting on shingles. None catching.
I keep going the rounds till 5 a.m.
when the wind fell.

8 Saturday.
Two men came through and told us
that Baudette was wiped out
and a good many
killed. The people gone
to Rainy River village.
We cut the road out
and watched fire all day.
Big fire around farm all night.

9 Sunday.
Been keeping the fire down
on clearing all day. Big fire south and east.

Maggie was at Rapid River and saw the settlers
coming in siding after night.

10 Monday.
I am at Maggie's house and intend
writing some letters.
Afternoon smoke so dense
cannot see half across River.

12 Wednesday.
Dry. Some heavy smoke,
blowing NW.
Maggie and Willie at Baudette.
Came on terrible lightning
and thunder there,
rain.

13 Thursday.
Rain all day.

14 Friday.
Took in the things
which was thrown out
in case of burning.

15 Saturday.
Cutting wood forenoon.
Rowed to Baudette.
Was all through the ruins.
Everything swept clean.
No timber left.

Then was over to Rainy River.
Ferry $.25,
Scotch $1.70,
Supper $.50,
Treats girls $.25,
1.25 for candy and fruit.
Day fine winds west.

17 Monday.
Cold and rainy. Evening.

18 Tuesday.
Snow 1/2 inch.

7. What Was Saved

At the last minute the wind turned away
and left the train depot and lumber mill
under a hail of cinders: the train
the only transportation left;
the mill busy for months with fire-struck timber.

At the last minute the wind turned away:
a few homesteads still blotched the landscape.
People gathered where there was a roof.
They tried to remember what a house looked like,
how to act when they went indoors.

What the fire left was clean and pure,
black and flat as the lake. It was possible to start
again, to take the emptiness and fill it
with memory and markers,
to drop down anchor.

8. Red Cross Houses

Scattered across ashy plots, they stood
tall and narrow on charred ground.

When a house was done,
the family at the top of the list moved in.

It didn't matter where we'd lived before:
the land belonged to everyone.

The list determined
where.

9. Before and After

On the top picture my mother has drawn
    an arrow aimed at a building on Main Street:
        Dad's Modern Pharmacy.

A long, dark building with a flat roof, it faces the bay
    next to a vacant lot. In the next picture,
        I can make out the same slight curve in the street

where it passed by the building, but now
    there is no building. The messy village
        is gone. What remains

is the dirt road that passed through and still passes,
    shortened by the vista. The fall of 1910:
        You can see great distances. Nothing stands

in the way. All the buildings are gone
    but the depot and sawmill. The branches
        of the trees, what few stand, have burned away.

All these erasures clear the view,
    so that people standing on one end of the county
        might hope to see their children standing on the other.

10. The Fourteen Unknown

Twenty-seven of the victims, only thirteen of which can now be identified, were buried in a mass grave at the Baudette Cemetery.
– "Lake of the Woods County History "

In the chaos and fear of typhoid
after the fire,
they buried twenty-seven people
together in a trench; fourteen of them

unnamed,
and no one knew for sure
who they were.

As a child, I used to visit them.
While my mother cut
the grass on my grandfather's grave,
I went down the hill to the monument,
to the indentation of earth

    where boats had landed
    with their loads of pine coffins,
    where the trench had curled up the hill
    from the Baudette River,

to the named people—

    William Jorgenson
    All the members of the Broten family
    The Goffins from Pitt

Kate Jasmick, a housekeeper who refused to leave her post
The six-day-old Dierkes infant who died of smoke inhalation
Mrs. Gust Larson—

and to those
buried
without names or mourners,
without flowers.

I think of the bones.
How they must have
slipped, an arm
slung across
another arm as the flesh dissolved,
loosened them.

How they might have crept together
down the hill: a face turned
toward another. How they might have
recognized each other
among the missing.

At Eight, When the House Burned

Walter Orr was burning trash that day: The sparks
came like a funnel cloud over the bay hill
and caught the roof flush. It smoldered quietly
before flames leapt into the tin pale sky.

I didn't know until I sneaked inside, afterwards,
how my house had died. The outside looked
the same. Inside, smoke quieted everything.

I imagined the winter shed at the cemetery,
where they stored the corpses until the ground
thawed, a door in a hillside: I saw bodies laid
on shelves, wrapped in blankets. My house
was dark inside, waiting for burial.

Winter came, instead; wind hissed indifferently
through stained red oak leaves. We moved
to the country, days full of bus rides,
nights longer than the river. In the mornings,
before light, my father played Patsy Cline
on the only radio station there was.

April Day

The beached rowboats lie neatly tilted
on their sides. Paint flakes from their keels.
Patches of ice glitter underneath, where the sun
doesn't go, and at the edges of the river
where the current won't reach.

The men scrape and sand, then slather each boat
with a layer of green paint the color of grass.
I tire quickly of boat painting and scramble up the bank
into the woods, where the air is still chilly,
and find the only green there: moss
that has lain under the snow, all winter
holding its memory of light.

The ground is uneven: hard and icy, or spongy
where the sun reached it. The smell of oak leaves
comes through the snow. The moss is quiescent,
like the boats, patient through winter, now uncovered.
I reach down to touch the soft tufts of its fabric

and gather a little pile of twigs, some still damp,
to make myself a fire in the lightlessness of the woods.
The fire stays small because the moss is alive
and the ground saturated: just a tiny ring
of blackness that snuffs out at its greening edges,
where spring encroaches.

Red Shift

October herds the leaves toward winter. I drive
north, over bridges, through red pine forests.
My mother is leaving the family house after 65 years
for a small, tidy apartment that requires no maintenance
and no anxiety. Not easily uprooted, she is still graceful.

Home is already gone when I get there: most
of the furniture removed, nothing has place any more.
In my room, only the white painted dresser
and the row of old, leaf-musty children's books.
Straight chairs in the living room line up
in front of the television. The kitchen table is piled
with dishes and pots and things she thinks we might want.

> *There is nothing I want.*
> *Nothing I want here.*

We empty the house: I spend a day in the basement
cleaning out my father's papers. Did I tell you he had no
personal things? No letters, no journal, no family photos—
his only handwriting on accounts payable/receivable, his flight
   logs.

"That green hat looks nice on your red hair," he said to me once,
although the hat was blue and the hair, I thought, light brown.

The house was once two: After the 1910 fire,
the Red Cross came and built small houses quickly.
Later, two fire houses combined: spacious, unexpected,
with extra corners. In 1958, an attic fire
damaged the interior. We didn't move back
for two years, and it was a different house, then.

Two houses make a divided family. My mother
was born nine months and 14 days
after the 1910 fire. Children sometimes
arrive to announce that someone died.

> *Tell me about the family fire,*
> *the one that was cold*
> *thick ice over the deep lake.*

I can't get the bottom drawer of my dresser open.
It warped from all those layers of white paint.
The place where the houses were connected
warped, too. It leaks in every rain, and all winter—
no matter how often it is fixed, the walls streak water
as they did after the fire.

Since we are leaving the dresser for the new owners,
I pry my way in. Nothing left but
a hot water bottle and an old yellow lace curtain.
I leave them and push the drawer hard.

Stars that are leaving

In my earliest dream, the living room floor turns
to quicksand: We leap from couch to chair
unable to touch our feet down. But my grandmother
is too old to leap, and she disappears beneath us.

Sometimes I wake unable to put my foot on the floor
of my dark room.

> *I remember: a fine sawdust,*
> *golden-colored.*
> *It can't hold anything up.*

My aunt, somehow adrenalin-charged, moved the piano,
a five-foot seven-inch Grand, as flecks of fire
began sifting down the staircase. Something heavy
like a piano might go through the floor all on its own.

turn red

I am not allowed to go inside, that year we live
in the country, and the house sits dark and full of dried smoke.
My father tells me I will fall through the floor.
But I know where the key is.

■ ■ ■

My father once had an old farmhouse in the woods,
taken in trade for a debt, where birch and poplar
saplings had grown so dense they turned the field
into a fence. There were horses, clumsy and inert:
two big gray Percherons, remnants of a farm.

He would prop us on them, our legs
doing the splits over their wide backs.
Their feet were as big as my head.

Who is telling this story?
Nobody lets me speak.

Even after the horses are gone, I come often
to this place in the woods
with my little brother and my autistic cousin.
To pick wild raspberries
and scare each other with stories
about the dark cellar, where we never
dare to go.

There is a lot of yellow light still, even though the trees
come nearer every year. Scraps of someone's life:
a cupboard full of dusty jars of raspberry jam.

It is not manageable.
It is one large fabric.
Cloth is made mostly of holes.

The barn has already fallen down:
My father is afraid
we will go through the floor.
He tells us not to go in the farmhouse.
He tells us to be afraid.
He tells us not to go in.

This is not my worst fear.
What I want isn't here.

"You are earth, earth, earth," an astrologer once told me.
I, who never
go into a dark basement.

One day, I take a dusty jar of preserves and drop it
on the floor. I just let it slip, and I like the way it smears.
On the wall, jam spreads radiantly
in large purple blotches. I love these stains
and I love my arm flung forward
in the slinging of something, like a stone,
and the dull sound of old glass
breaking, muffled by jam.

My cousin and brother join in, we finish the jam jars.
A pole goes through the walls—they give way
easily, stump-rotted on the inside.
The shredded yellow curtains float out
of the upstairs window like bits of parachute,
catch on twigs and hang in the close trees.

Red is the color

But the floor holds. It has not rotted like the walls.
We break everything, but not the floor.
We can't break the floor.

> *You should stop talking.*
> *There are things*
> *you shouldn't say.*

I never went upstairs after the fire, to the place
where there was a hole

in the roof
and the fire had leaked through.

of going away

Now the piano sits submissively
in the apartment building's game room.
I have it tuned before I leave. Built in 1899, it doesn't keep
a tune long anymore.

■ ■ ■

Since his father died, my autistic cousin won't return.
Houses never held him here.
Broken houses never asked him to piece them back together.

■ ■ ■

Although there are still boxes piled up against
the living room wall, we lock the door and leave.
The benefit auction people will come on Monday
to take the rest. I can drive away now.

The houses have become quite silent—
The houses seem to have drifted—
The houses are shifting—

Stars that are leaving turn red, they say.
Red is the color of going away.

Depth of Field

In the Chippewa National Forest, at the continental divide,
there is a field of trees so deep it has almost fallen into dream.

Under red pines, the forest service has cut away the brush,
and late September, late afternoon light sifts a cloud

of pollen into this rapt woods. Trees catch
the light so far back you can see nearly to creation—

shafts push into the blue, certain autumn sky.
And you are aware of nothing

cutting through the poles of light.

Let Them

Why should all these old ones be sexless?
They are like us, only closer.

Lashed to the small boats of mortality,
they rock alone in an endless sea.

And so what if, at night, those who can,
climb into bed with each other?

The heart is always the last to go.

So if they want to hold each other, let them:
You know the size of darkness.

Afraid to Look Afraid
to Look Away

Moonlight breaks on the fir trees
in the deep forest
she waits for you.

The garden of stones casts
shadows
hover on the ground.

The breadcrumbs are
the old trail
of pebbles is white in

the moonlight
has no beginning.

Leave this false trail
and all trails:

Walk toward what
you don't know
the moon will take you there.

The house is
gingerbread and sugar
will fill you up at first.

You will think you
have found childhood.

But she is inside
what you eat
devours you.

Stay with her, let her feed you
as she will
stoke her oven.

Keep your brother safe from
her dim eyes
cannot see you.

Wait for her to go to
the fire
will move you.

You must stay and
watch her burn if you forget
and look away

you will forget.

Now the fire burns on
in the garden
you wake the stones.

Has Been Seen

Can't remember, and imagines.
Like eggs in a nest, puts cheek to quick.
And sleeps.
Watches over.

Like an old enemy, with intimacy.
In missed doorways, the shape of the light.
What should enter.
What should alter.

Like a fox that has been seen, and fixes
an eye upon you.
Appears to approach
is backing away. Is gone.

September Frost Warning

1.

Last night after the sun went down
we covered the raspberries—
so many still ripening,
the plastic sheets rigid from sudden cold,
full of rain pockets—
and walking back to the house, found
the sugar maple still holding
light from the day pulsing gold
incandescent in the blackening dusk
and we held each other's cold muddy hands
as we stood near the beams of the tree
and heard how the heart
keeps time
and takes it.

2.

A third eye propels the birds
south, toward the sun:
it empties the sky.

Seat of the nut-sized soul,
pineal remnant of all
our desire,

where will you send us
now that the sun is
going away?

What are you
the trace of,
what have you left

in us, imprint
of what lost eden
toward which we

strain to fly?

3.

I am listening for you—
the voice I hear everywhere,
underneath the car tires,
the road, the high wind
bringing October to the trees,
the quiet hissing of leaves
as green recedes. The silence
left behind as the birds go south,
the sloping light that replaces them.
All that is falling away
is in your voice. I am listening,
listening, and my bones
have become dense
with the music.

4.

Before the leaves fall,
before they gather

into senseless little flocks
to wander the roads,

just as they turn
to face the departing sun,

I think of walking
through rooms cluttered
with light,

I think of sitting
in your green chair

by the window,
spilled yellowness
on my hands.

I try to hold it,
cupping,

curling my fingers in.

5.

All summer snowy egrets fish the ponds and ditches.
When September sets the world on edge, they leave
one by one and the sky stays light—
no shadows pass.

All summer I watch, but never catch that moment
when they leave. Days later, I realize, as if
someone's breathing had stopped,
the sky is empty.

The Bare Minimum

Facing north, the winter trees
branch like pure syntax:
skeletal and dense.

Baby owls lie bare
and pallid in winter nests,
their eyes black under translucent,
unopened lids—

the dark tumors on their throats
are not death, but regurgitated
mouse flesh.

The great horned ones turn and call
and call themselves
and night.
Each has a twin who also calls.

Each has a listener in the dark
who wakes and hears
her own voice,
another barely remembered,

thin and bloodless, rasping
against the window
the way a bare maple branch
breaks from its hinge.

From Home

People go away from home to see.

Waves threshing the shore.
Time laps.

Water and sky fold on each other.
A trick of geometry.

The ship leaving Taconite Harbor.
Suddenly slips over.

How it is for the spider to come to an empty web.

Source

After a night's rain, this rivulet runs loudly to the lake
and, in the pool where rock slows the water,
one dark minnow hides from my shadow under a ledge.

I dip my fingers in to see if it's rain runoff, but the water is cold,
too cold for August rainwater, and sweet: Somewhere up there
a spring yields this stream from the deep ground

and I want to follow, go back up the hill on slippery
mossy rocks through greeny twigs and yellowing saplings
that grasp at my hair, to find the place where

this water leaves the earth. If I were alone, that's what
I'd do. But you call me back to the lake, and I slide down
to the mouth of the stream, where a small child has played,

used thin sticks as bridges between the tiny islands of rock,
placed two larger stones and two small ones—a family?—near one
   bridge;
when you call me, I come, even though my desire

goes back to where this water enters
the world through a cleft in rock and makes its way down
to the bridgeless, indistinguishable waters of the lake.

On Two

The mind splits
without much difficulty
a natural act.

> Twins: *a compound crystal*
> *composed of two or more crystals—*
> *or parts of crystals—*
> *of the same kind that are grown together*
> *in a specific manner.*

Can you see them?
Composed, parts, same, specific manner—
If I close my eyes and think
of nothing, I might see crystals
in their petri dishes going on
with the process of dupleness
and interfering with it.

Two is a field of opposites.
You and I are digging there.
A third is between us. She waits for us to find her.
She may be a sunflower
on a tall stalk turning her head
above. She may be a potato,
many-eyed beneath our feet.

Keep looking, I say to you.
Connection is bittersweet. That
will split the mind.

But two always wants to go to three:
once two, a third is possible.
This is a kind of reproductive
law of the mind.

With one, three can never be.
Who is willing
to look into *miles on miles of nought*
to find the thing we dig for?
Then again, who is willing to forego
twoness? (If something else
attracts us more.)

I've tried to stand still on the sharp two
of paradox, but it's only when
the third rises
that I stop falling:

the axe
in the oak, its flight
and the cleft of its landing;
the picture of oneself standing on the stairs
getting ready to fly;
the train ticket with number 55 on it
and the decision to let go
of whatever one holds in one's hands.

By which I mean mine, of course.
Two is a field
of connection, your hands
and mine. I don't like to speak

of emotions. They travel behind me
in pairs. I am the third, a crowd.
They have names like *compound, composed, specific.*
They are like explaining colors
to a blind person. Some of the blind
have learned to hear colors, I've read.

There are only two
things: time and eternity, the twins
of the double mind. Eros is the corpus callosum:
Eros is the third.
The broker. Now I have said it.

I do not believe in wholeness.
I believe that *women should be skeptical of mirrors,*
that twinge is the plural of twin.

I promise never to confuse you with anyone else.

Divided

Sometimes I think it is the fox
coming toward me down the path—
we are both looking elsewhere

when we meet. Our eyes stand still
searching for something familiar
I think I find but then the fox

turns. Or I think it is the owl
and the night belongs to her, not
to me: she leaves bones in the woods,

I wake up weightless, compact.
And sometimes I think it is you—
I have carried you up into these hills

that haul the wash of April
in their arms. You are light,
just a sac of dried-up

bones that I scatter into the wind
like winter leaves, or like a promise
I have always meant to keep.

Amherst Winter

1.

All that she thought nested in winter.
The turned-over soil, resting black and white in the spare
New England sun. Her sister, creaking below
on the uneven wooden floors
in constant motion, enough
to keep her own stillness.

The windows crystalline from the edges,
oval mirror
at the center. Bread smells
filling the stairwell, a cylindrical core of heat.
The palms of the hands, fingers open,
memory of kneading.

Storm in the trees rattling them like glass
on the cupboard shelf. Sometimes she, too, would break
into music, if she couldn't help herself, touching
the piano's keys, white and black.
But most of the time she held her fingers
curled tight.

> *The things of which we want the proof*
> *are those we knew before.*

2.

No longer ask to relinquish love
nor keep it under glass.

Let your heart be wild and full
of grief.

Keep no distances—

not for peace nor for serenity
nor for release.

Give nothing for renunciation.

See the one who sees
you: Greet your particular solitude.

Be grateful for all that
you do not have.

Enlarge it.

> *Great Hungers feed themselves,*
> *but little Hungers ail in vain.*

3.

I leave it on my windowsill,
the spider I don't kill
or put outside:
There's snow, now.

I like to watch it motionless
until something catches
in the snarl, shakes the web
and slides it out of stillness,

fast and purposeful—not hasty
to the quarry:
A late wasp, trapped by warmth
in the walls, now at this window

where the golden spider, large
as a quarter, tames
its hunger by waiting,
tames the wasp with poison.

At my desk I'm close enough
to hear the sound of spider
tearing the brittle-bodied
wasp apart.

Shaking with its maker's efforts,
the big web, attached
beyond the window to the wall
and the beam above my chair, keeps growing.

Winter unwinds and the spider waits.
At night I see it hanging
in the web,
legs extended,

floating, attached by a single
line
at the abdomen.
Nothing's in the web.

Retreating to the window frame,
the spider is still for days.
The web slackens. I can't tell the difference
between watchfulness and death.

> *Amalgams are abundant, but the lone student*
> *of the Mines adores Alloyless things.*

4.

She felt most at home going away.
She felt most herself estranged.

She let everything seek its level:
She compressed her life.

She was light and dense
and she carried everything with her.

She sent doubt out to gather her friends
from wherever they were

and bring them to the circle
of her immense craving.

> *To the faithful Absence is condensed presence,*
> *To others—but there are no others—*

Conversation with My Father

Time has expanded between us.
- Marie Ponsot

She keeps putting more soil and seed on:
The grass doesn't want to grow.

Five years, and still she heaps up mounds
of black dirt, sprinkles the grass seed in April
and again in September, for the cool and rain.

Each time I visit, I hope she's failed again.
I want to see that dark scar of dirt,

not the green swale of an old grave.
What she wants to cover up, I want
to remember:

you finally saying *I love you*
on your ninetieth birthday,
the way you'd leave us behind,

forget promises, find other
things to do.

Now there is plenty of time

on this rise next to the gravel county road
and the shallow butt end of the river,
with the cows looking on.

I will sit and listen
to the cattle lowing

and your silence, that ongoing voice,
the one I've always heard.

Novitiate

1. Spinning

Whipping on the clothesline
in the late autumn Red River Valley wind,
the dresses, black and white,
have been dismembered in the laundry room,
the velcro stripped by tiny
Sister Angelique, whose job it is
to part the collar from the black
swath of wool.

The wind of anamnesis weaves fragments
on a loom with wool; the threads spin
a slender line
to Sister Angelique who,
ancient face alight,
still separates the black from white.

2. Shudder

You stand in a frisson of fire,
the day breaking across your face
as if this were your first sunrise.
She stares at your edges, outlined
in pulses of light; she does not see
you, the mother who lives in another
universe, in which you
do not entirely exist.

3. The Pump Room

There is a place within convent walls
that runs like ice across a summer sweat.
We go there, summer days, after working in the fields,
to slake our thirst, but more, to get our spirits wet.
The tin cup hangs on the dripping pipe,
dented, tangy with metallic zest.
We pump, we bring up streams of hope
that overflows our cups, our weariness.
So many hours of bending in the field,
so many piles of corn to husk and cut
away the worms and blight; we've peeled
too many apples, cored too many centers out.
But then the water comes up slowly: cold
and pure from dark rivers far below.

4. Roman Road

The priest sang in a bleating voice
like the sheep milling at the dining room
windows, their noses pressed to glass.
They watched us eat their kin.

He was deaf and old, but still
robust and big, and he worked hard
outdoors to keep his unruly
body tamed among all the women.

He built a road, a raised highway
through the woods, and called it high
Latin names: Appian Way, Iter Mirabile. It was
the Roman Road, built with his ithyphallic sweat.

He planted saplings on the hillside, scrawny
fruit trees that never bore anything,
not even a late apple. He could not hear
our confessions, but he absolved.

5. Stained Glass

Voices rise from the light flooding
across the tile of the chapel floor.
The Way of the Cross colors the day.

Early, The Crowning of Thorns
cascades through the east windows
in ripples of green and gold.

At noon, The Crucifixion shimmers
in white, simple light that falls direct
on the head of the bowed Christ.

In the afternoon sun's slope, incense drifts
across pillars of blue and yellow light:
the women gathering the bodies of Christ.

6. All I Remember Now

All I remember now is the churning
of the seasons, the colors of the chapel air
shifting with the light, the leaves, the smell
of dead leaves in fall and the way they fired
spark-risen against a deep sky.

All I remember now is the singing, the way
the sound continued like a heartbeat resonating
through the silence, the treble voices stooping
under the round, blue ceiling of their range,
my own voice switching from soprano to second
and back to fill the cracks between bigger,
better voices, the sudden moment
in which the voices coalesce and become one.

All I remember now is the empty rooms, the leavings
of old ones who died, murmuring their last prayers
in French, counting the novices *un deux trois quatre*,
the places where women once had been that now
were empty, the places where I had been that now are empty,
and the silence that has released me.

Landscape: Western Minnesota

Light rises on the fields turning in their dreams.
Early spring: an unseasonable thaw leaves
burlap and gold stubble, or turned-over
black from fire the year before.
There is no green, but every hill shines
under the March sun's incline. Ice rots
on the ponds, deep blue, as if the sky
had gotten underneath this emptiness,
edge of prairie, the fallow idleness
of landscape caught in sleep.
Now it comes out of winter sluggish and unspeakable,
pulling memory behind it, team
of horses hauling a load of last year's hay.

Winter Necessities

At night, now that darkness keeps
the soil and rain hardens into a pillar
of winter, an owl has come into the woods
to hoot quietly, persistent and soft,
black limb and white ground.

It may have been the birds we feed
that drew it to the falling shadows
of oak and box elder: Now it stays
the season, conversing
with the fragile bones of finches and mice.

All along, the mind knew that it had been taken
into this conversation, into the slender
parcel of these small deaths,
all along considering these necessities
in the sidelong glance of winter light.

Ripening

Globes of thistle
loosen at the frayed ends
of their spikes and let go, clouds drifting purple
over a yellow field.

I've come
to find their guardians,
the summer-voiced goldfinches who do not sow,
but wait

on the thin stems of wild oats
for the harvest—black, shiny pods gliding slender
as snow.

I've come
to find a way
into the wild tongue of the thistle

that scours the river
of drowned light, that climbs
through the windy sky and the heaviness.

Fireflies

Like flickers of intuition,
on a certain night in June, after rain,

they begin flight, one by one, gathering
over the tall grass in the ditch.

You think you mistook the random flash
of light. You think you saw a reflection

of the long outspread day slipping away,
or maybe the beginning of a summer

storm—the dart of lightning so far
off there is no rumble of thunder.

No: Do not mistake the fireflies
for anything else. Concede

the way they stretch you past
what you were, that sudden flare.

Notes

Page xiii: The epigraph is taken from Rita Dove's poem "Freedom Ride," in her book *On the Bus with Rosa Parks*, published by W. W. Norton & Company. Used by permission.

Page 7: "1910" is based on research about a forest fire that swept what is now Lake of the Woods County in Northern Minnesota, killing many settlers and destroying towns and villages. My mother's family survived this fire. A special note of appreciation to Marlys Hirst of the Lake of the Woods County Historical Society and to the *Baudette Region* for help with the 1910 fire information and photographs.

Page 13: Section 6, "David Coutts," is a found poem taken from an unpublished diary that recounts the events of the 1910 fire.

Page 19: The epigraph is from a locally published book about the county by the Lake of the Woods County Historical Society, 1997. The article on the fire is by Elnora Bixby and Florence Ferrier.

Page 34: The title, "Afraid to Look Afraid to Look Away," is taken from the last line of a poem by Eleanor Wilner.

Page 46: The line *miles on miles of nought* is a quotation from Emily Dickinson's poem, "I Tie my Hat – I crease my Shawl – (number 522, Franklin).

Page 47: The italicized phrase *women should be skeptical of mirrors* is a statement from Joan Retallack. I have been unable to identify the exact source.

Page 51: The last two lines of each section of "Amherst Winter" are quotations from *The Letters of Emily Dickinson*, edited by Thomas H. Johnson, published by The Belknap Press.

Page 56: The epigraph is taken from Marie Ponsot's poem "We Are Imagined," in her book *The Bird Catcher*, published by Alfred A. Knopf.

Acknowledgments

The author and publisher gratefully acknowledge the following
publications in which some of the poems in this book first
appeared—

Concrete Wolf: "Landscape: Western Minnesota"

Crania: "Divided"

Diner: "Conversation with My Father" and "Fireflies"

Great River Review: "Novitiate"

The Laurel Review: "Depth of Field"

Poet Lore: "Source"

The Poets' Grimm: 20th Century Poems from Grimm Fairy Tales,
edited by Jeanne Marie Beaumont and Claudia Carlson (Story
Line Press, 2003): "Afraid to Look Afraid to Look Away"

Prairie Schooner: "The Arsonist," "The Trees Turn," "Fire Eater,"
and "September Frost Warning"

Shenandoah: "Winter Necessities"

Grateful thanks, also, to Janet Holmes, John Reinhard, Joan
Aleshire, Anne Carson, Claudia Rankine, Eleanor Wilner, Betty
Adcock, Constance Merritt, and the Wednesday night writers:
Becca Barniskis, Amy McNamara, Mary Jo Thompson, and Susan
Steger Welsh.

About the Author

A native of Northern Minnesota, Kathleen Jesme continues to live in her home state on a small tree farm near St. Paul. She earned her MFA degree from Warren Wilson College and is a self-employed training consultant. Her poetry appears in *Prairie Schooner, Shenandoah, The Laurel Review, Great River Review, Poet Lore,* and other journals and anthologies.

About the Book

Fire Eater is set in Janson types based on fonts originally designed in about 1690 by Nicholas Kis, a Hungarian typefounder, punchcutter, and printer working in Amsterdam. A modern version was prepared for the Linotype Company under the direction of C. H. Griffith in the 1930s and it was adapted and released for digital composition by Adobe Systems in 1988. Richard Mathews designed and typeset the book, decorated with his flame ornaments, at the University of Tampa Press. It has been printed on acid-free Glatfelter Supple Opaque Natural recycled text papers, with printing and binding by Fidlar Doubleday of Kalamazoo, Michigan.